PIANO • VOCAL

GLORIA ESTEFAN
THE STANDARDS

gloriaestefan.com

facebook.com/gloriaestefan

twitter.com/gloriaestefan

CONTENTS

Alfred

Produced by
Alfred Music
P.O. Box 10003
Van Nuys, CA 91410-0003
alfred.com

Printed in USA.

ISBN-10: 1-4706-1038-8
ISBN-13: 978-1-4706-1038-8

Cover Artwork by Jesus Cordero • *Special Thanks to Shelly Berg for his Orchestrations*

GOOD MORNING HEARTACHE

Words and Music by
ERVIN DRAKE, DAN FISHER
and IRENE HIGGINBOTHAM

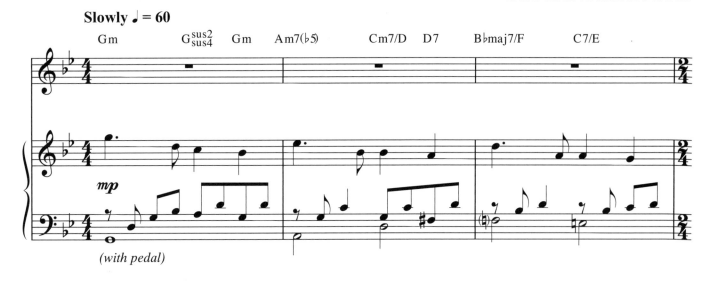

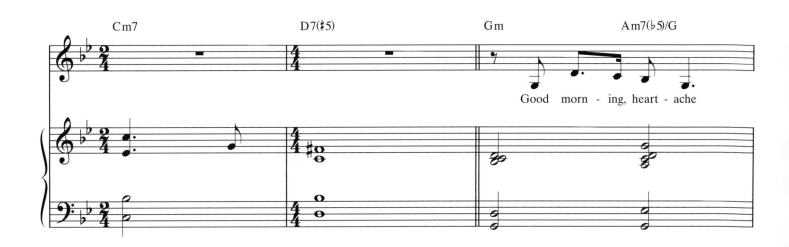

Good morn-ing, heart-ache

you old___ gloom-y sight. Good morn-ing heart-ache, thought we said good-bye last night.

Good Morning Heartache - 6 - 1

4

6

THEY CAN'T TAKE THAT AWAY FROM ME

Music and Lyrics by
GEORGE GERSHWIN and IRA GERSHWIN

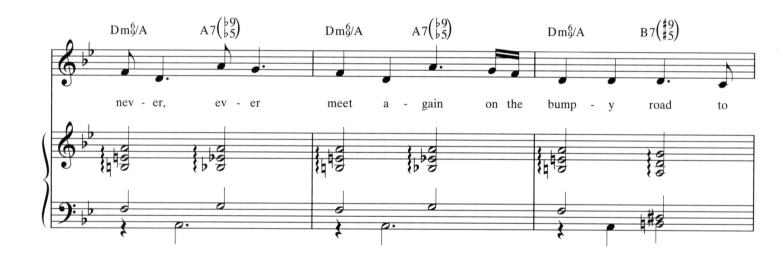

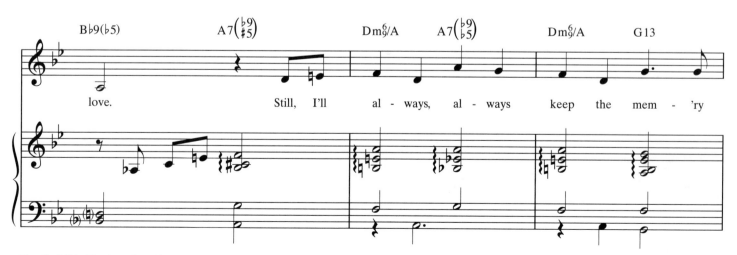

They Can't Take That Away From Me - 11 - 1

14

WHAT A DIFFERENCE A DAY MAKES

Words by
STANLEY ADAMS

Music by
MARIA GREVER

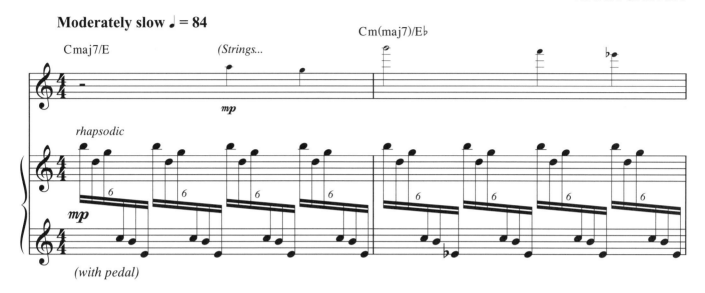

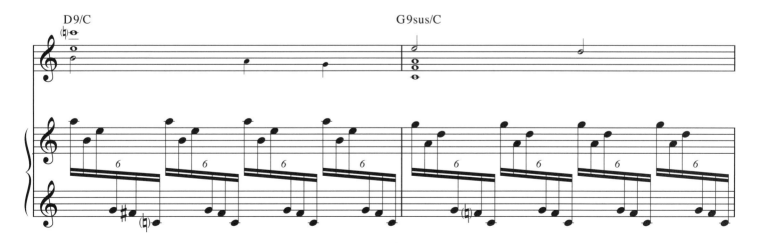

22

I'VE GROWN ACCUSTOMED TO HIS FACE

Words by
ALAN JAY LERNER

Music by
FREDERICK LOEWE

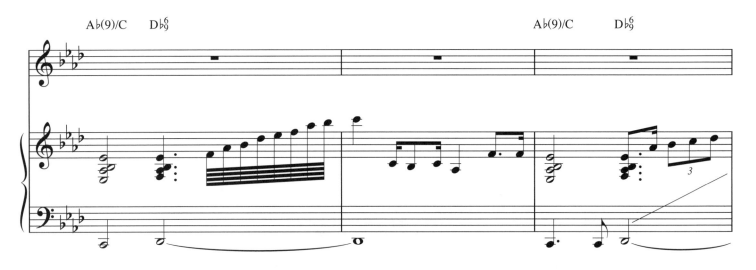

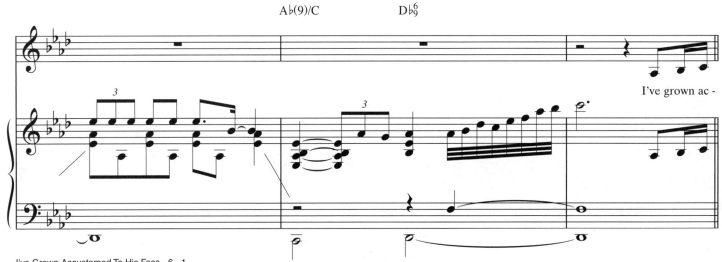

I've grown ac -

32

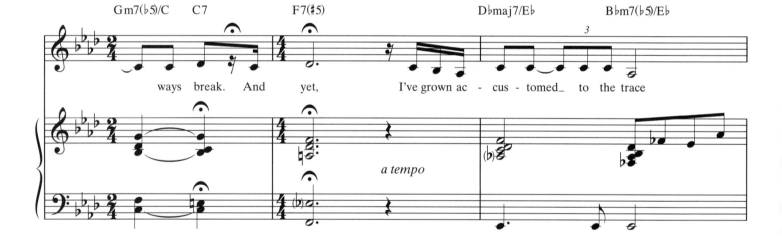

EU SEI QUE VOU TE AMAR

Words by
VINICIUS DE MORAES

Music by
ANTONIO CARLOS JOBIM

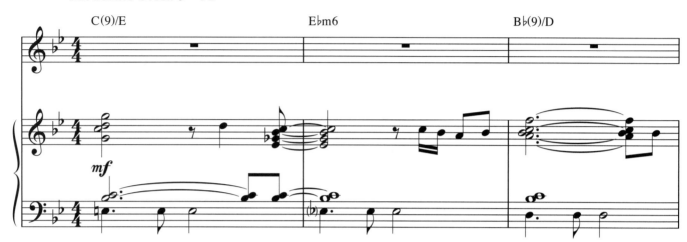

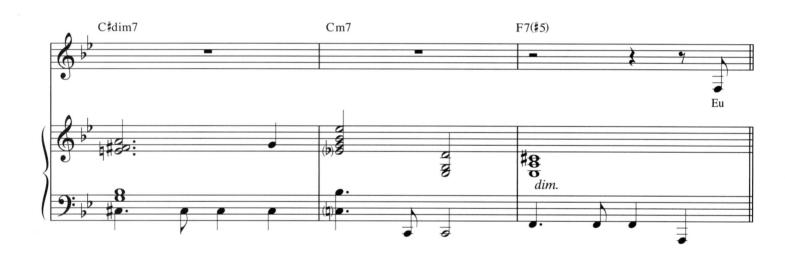

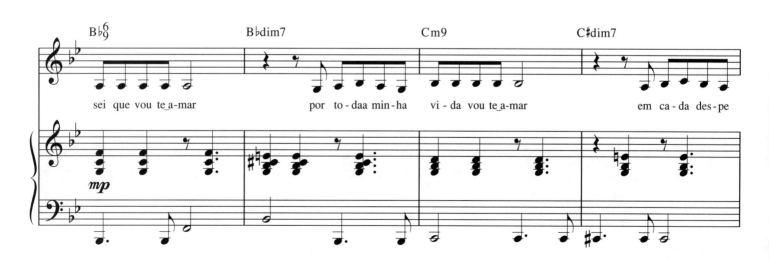

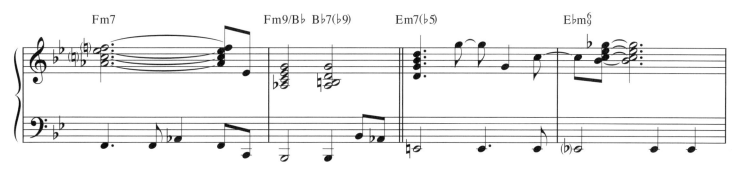

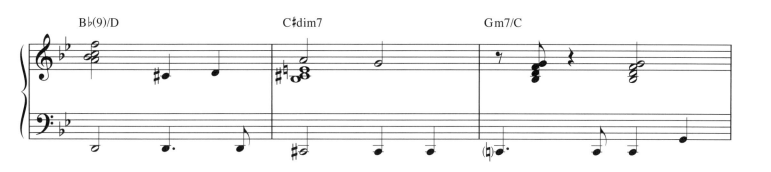

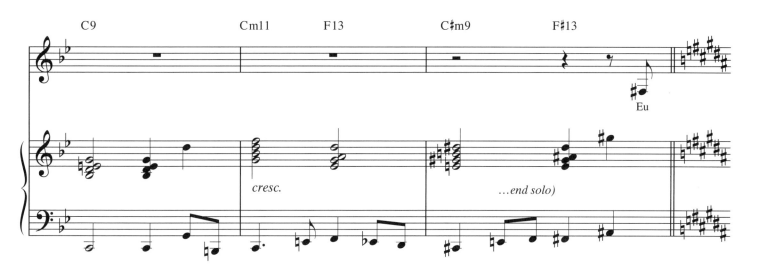

...end solo)

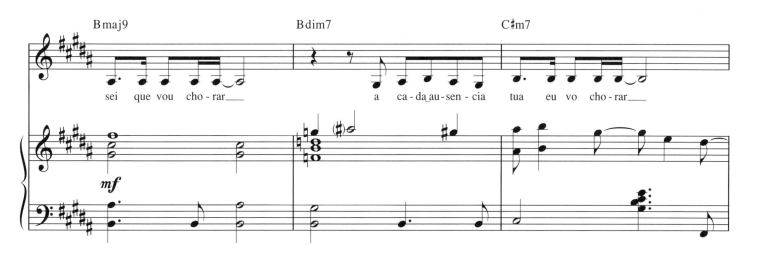

sei que vou cho-rar___ a ca-da au-sen-cia tua eu vo cho-rar___

THE DAY YOU SAY YOU LOVE ME

Words by
ALFREDO LE PERA
English Lyrics by
GLORIA M. ESTEFAN

Music by
CARLOS GARDEL

Slowly, but freely (♩ = 80)

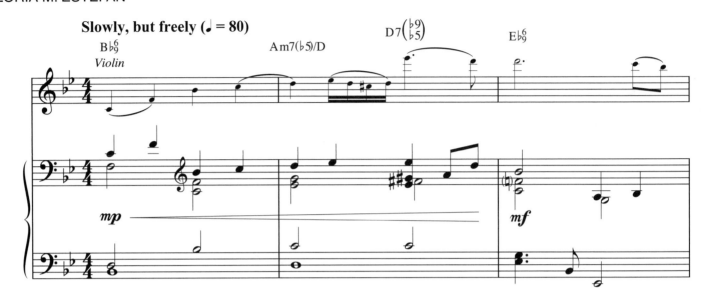

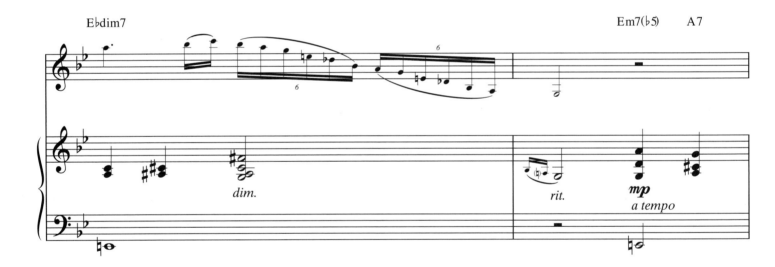

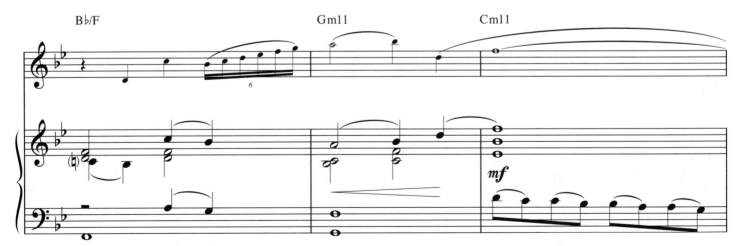

The Day You Say You Love Me - 8 - 1

The Day You Say You Love Me - 8 - 4

44

46

Slightly faster, but freely

al - ways trea - sure.

EMBRACEABLE YOU

Music and Lyrics by
GEORGE GERSHWIN
and IRA GERSHWIN

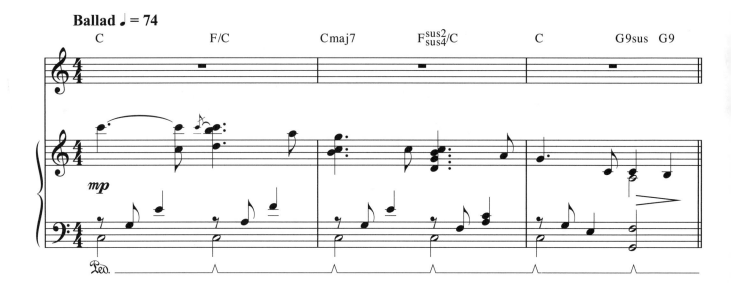

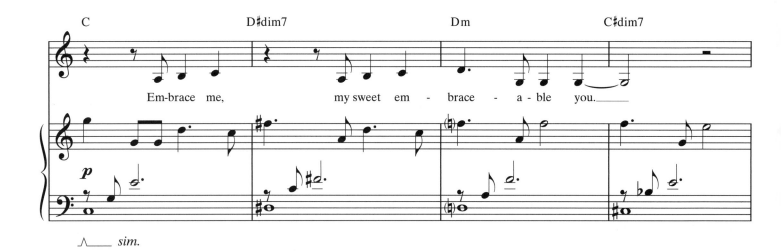

Em-brace me, my sweet em - brace - a - ble you.

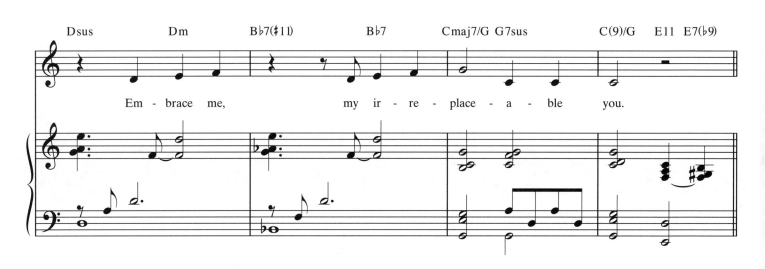

Em - brace me, my ir - re - place - a - ble you.

Embraceable You - 5 - 1

52

WHAT A WONDERFUL WORLD

Words and Music by
GEORGE DAVID WEISS and BOB THIELE

Moderately slow and expressive ♩ = 74

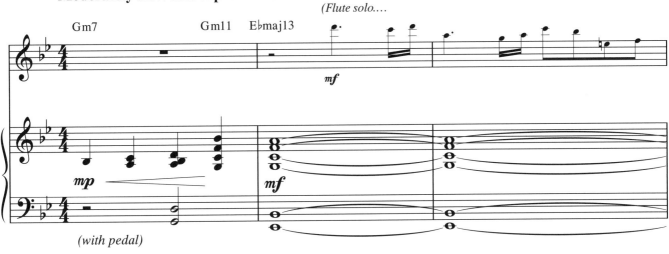

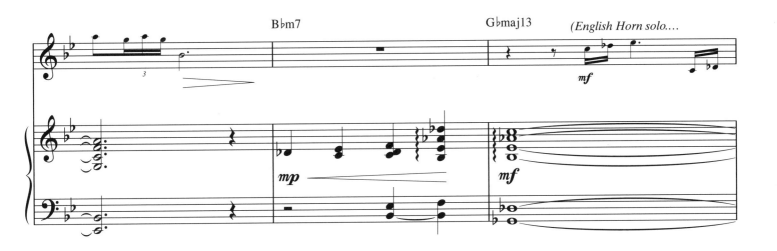

What A Wonderful World - 7 - 1

54

58

They're real - ly say - ing, "I love you!"

I gear ba - bies cry,____

I____ watch them grow. They'll learn much more

than I'll ev - er____ know. And I think to my - self,____

What A Wonderful World - 7 - 6

CALL ME IRRESPONSIBLE

Words by
SAMMY CAHN

Music by
JAMES VAN HEUSEN

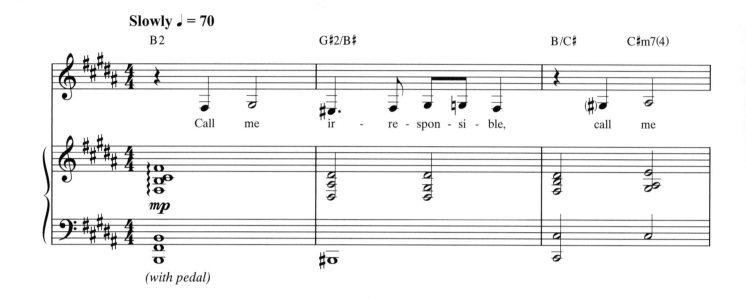

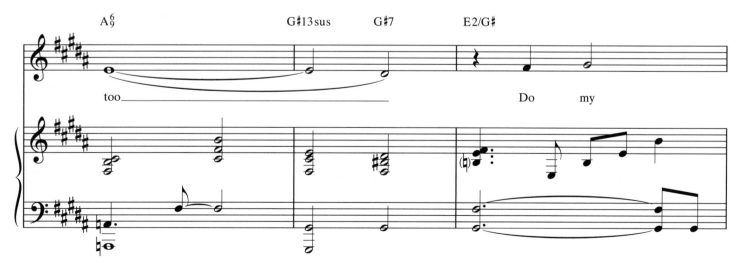

Call Me Irresponsible - 8 - 1

64

HOW LONG HAS THIS BEEN GOING ON?

Lyrics by
IRA GERSHWIN

Music by
GEORGE GERSHWIN

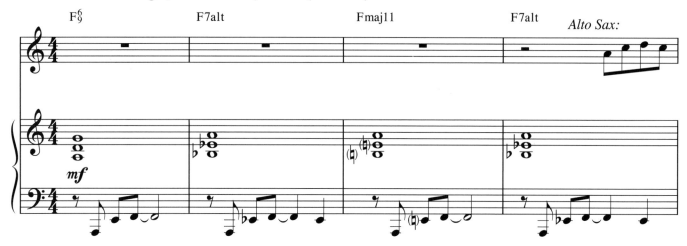

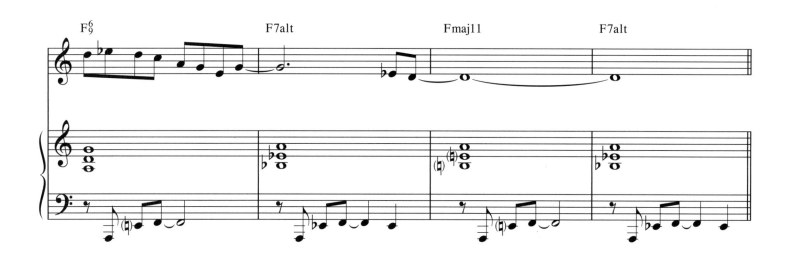

Refrain:

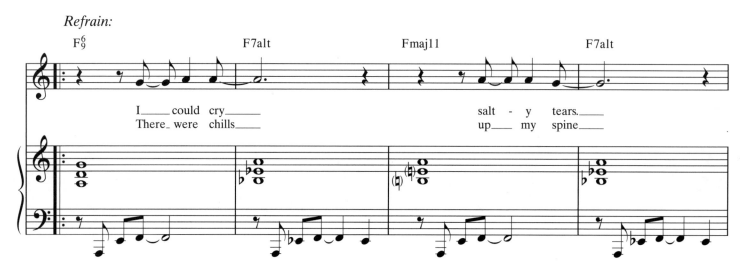

I____ could cry____ salt - y tears.____
There_ were chills____ up__ my spine____

How Long Has This Been Going On? - 8 - 1

74

THE WAY YOU LOOK TONIGHT

Words by
DOROTHY FIELDS

Music by
JEROME KERN

Moderate bossa ♩ = 140

Lyrics:

Some - day____ when I'm aw - f'ly low,____
Love - ly,____ with your smile so warm,_

and the world is cold,____
and your cheeks so soft,____

I will feel a glow____ just think - ing of
there is noth - ing for____ me but to love

The Way You Look Tonight - 8 - 4

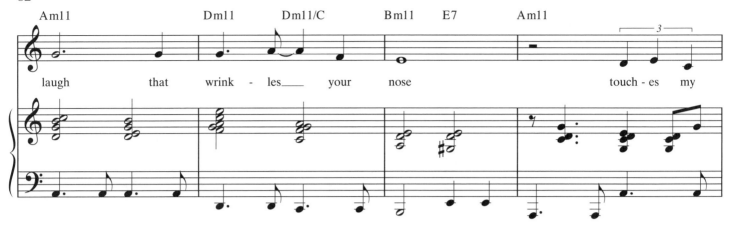

laugh that wrink - les___ your nose touch - es my

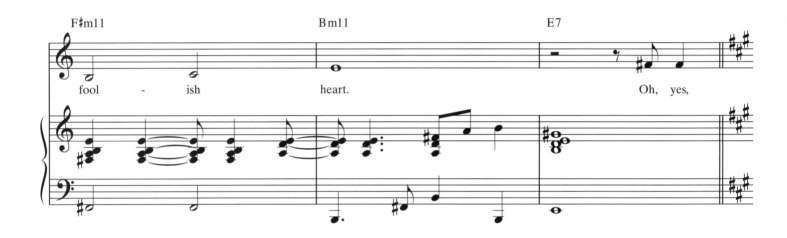

fool - ish heart. Oh, yes,

love - ly,___ nev - er ev - er change,___

keep that breath - less charm,___

YOU MADE ME LOVE YOU
(I DIDN'T WANT TO DO IT)

Words by
JOE McCARTHY

Music by
JAMES V. MONACO

Afro-Cuban ♩ = 192

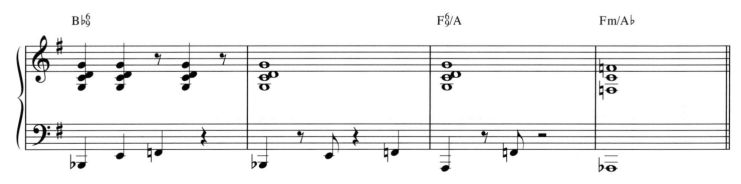

You Made Me Love You - 8 - 1

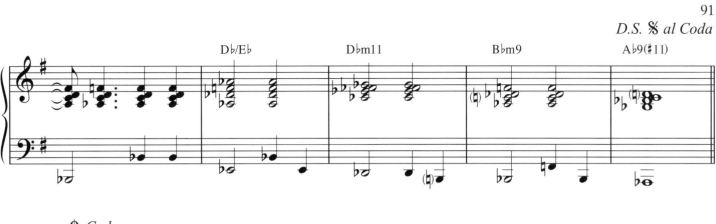

⊕ *Coda*

you.

Repeat as desired, vocal ad-lib.

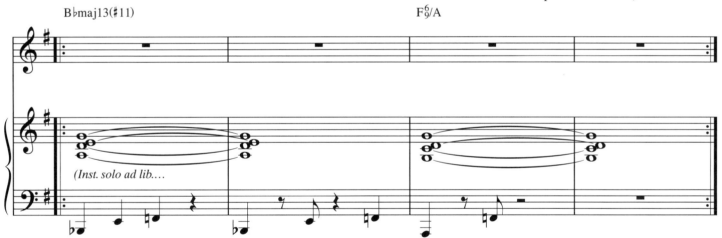

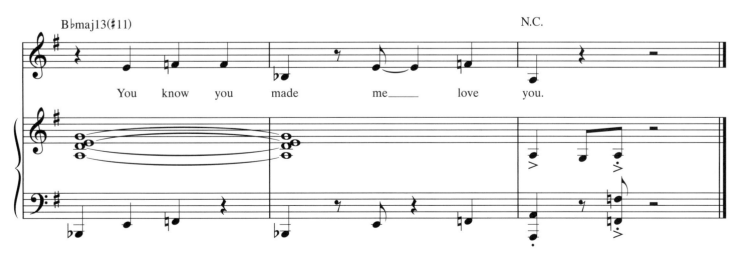

You know you made me____ love you.

FOR ALL WE KNOW

Words by
SAM M. LEWIS

Music by
J. FRED COOTS

For All We Know - 6 - 1

YOUNG AT HEART

Words by
CAROLYN LEIGH

Music by
JOHNNY RICHARDS

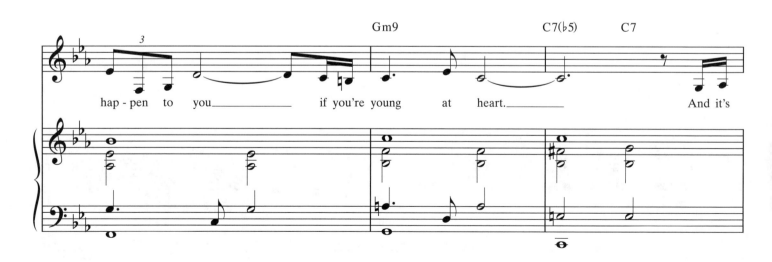

Young At Heart - 6 - 1

here is the best part, you have a head start if you are a-mong the ver - y young at

Faster ♩ = 128

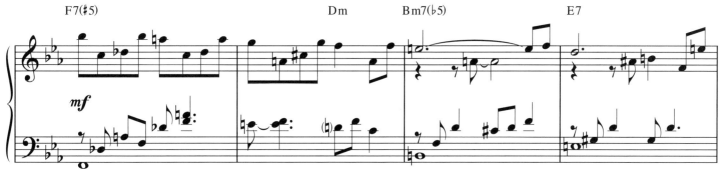

heart.

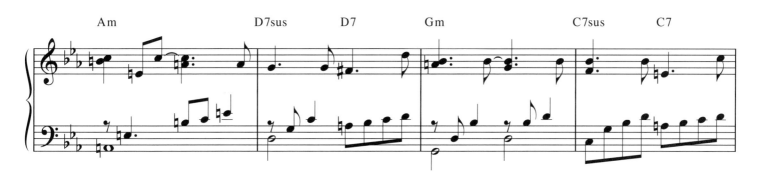

Tempo I

Fm11

Don't you know that it's worth ev-ry treas-ure on earth_____ to be

Gm11   C7(♭5)   C7   Fm11

young   at   heart._____   For as   rich_____   as you are   it's much

Fm9/B♭   B♭9   E♭(9)   F/E♭   E♭maj7

bet-ter   by   far_____   to be   young   at   heart._____   And if

Gm7(♭5)   C7(♭9)   Gm7(♭5)   C7(♯5)   Fm11   Fm9

you_____   should sur-vive_____   to a   hun-dred and five,   think of   all   you'll de-rive   out of

cresc.

SONRÍE

Words by
JOHN TURNER and **GEOFFREY PARSONS**
Spanish Lyric Adaptation by
GLORIA M. ESTEFAN

Music by
CHARLES CHAPLIN

Ballad ♩ = 82

(with pedal)

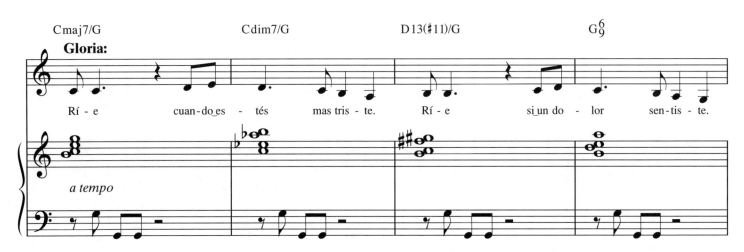

Gloria:

Rí - e cuan-do_es - tés mas tris - te. Rí - e si_un do - lor sen - tis - te.

a tempo

Sonríe - 5 - 1

108